A Hiccup in a Tea Cup

by

Shaine Singer

A Hiccup in a Tea Cup

By Shaine Singer

ISBN: 9780993300837

All Rights Reserved.

Copyright © Shaine Singer 2016

Cover Design by Garry Vaux

www.GJBpublishing.co.uk

This book is sold subject to the condition that it shall not, by way of trade or otherwise, be re-sold or otherwise circulated without the publisher's prior consent in any form or binding other than that in which it is published. No part of this book may be replicated without the publisher's prior permission.

Contents

A Hiccup in a Tea Cup....7
In Memory of Liz....8
For Rescued Hedgehogs....9
Lorraine....10
Cats & Dogs....11
Valentines Day....12
Wonky Donkey....13
First Kiss....14
Jelly & Ice Cream....15
Jam & Toast....16
Cadbury's Dairy Milk....17
Hippos....18
The Undateables....19
Ode to First Dates....20
Autumn Leaves....21
An Ode to Bath....22
Isla Fisher....23
Oh Candy....24
Clocks....26
The Snowman That Likes to Ski....27
A Revolution....28
Dreams Within A Dream....29
Love Thous is Strange....31
What If....32
Natalie Wood....33
Ava Gardner....34

The Penny Farthing Bicycle....36
Things That Go Bump In The Night....37
The Sky At Night....39
Time....40
The TARDIS....41
If I Were A Timelord....42
The Fisher King....43
The Weeping Angels....44
Dementia & Alzheimers....46
Kate Beckinsale....48
Zygons....50
The Avengers....51
Sunday Roasts....53
Shrove Tuesday....54
If I Were King For A Day....55
Fun At The Fair....56
Four Leaf Clover....57
Hallowe'en....58
Love Bugs....59
Laughter....60
The Big Yellow Duck....61
The Man on the Moon....62
The Naughty Christmas Elf....63
The Pig in the Wig....64

I want to thank friends,

family and fans throughout the year.

Enjoy!

A Hiccup In A Teacup

When you drink a cup of tea, it's pleasant, lovely,
But it isn't nice when you have hiccups.
It's a strange pick me up when you have a hiccup in a teacup,
Then you go beep n burp, oops pardon me, burp, hiccup, splish splash,
Take a deep breath or have a glass of water,
Try not to go hiccup or burp with so many muddled words and
Spluttering, wet face of hiccupped water everywhere,
Almost like a puddle of hiccups.
So be careful when you have hiccups,
Never drink tea with a hiccup in a teacup.

In Memory Of Liz

Liz was a triumph a great personality,
Bubbly bundle of joy,
Quirky and bright, funny,
Great admin for Double Act.
She rocked.
A great inspiration to all who knew her.
She was like a belle of the ball.
Singer in a choir, joyful companion,
Disability activist, colleague.
Will sorely miss her.
She brought cheer and honey
Melancholic moments everywhere.

For Rescued Hedgehogs

(For A Friend - To a Star of Sara Hogspital)

A lady of bliss and calm,
Bundle of joy, happy and fun,
Smart, lovely lady Sara,
A belle, you sure are friends.
Wandering star,
You're going far,
Their names are Paul & Nancy,
Friendly, wild hedgehogs,
Little creatures with unique features,
Beauty, wise, wisdom, calm, collective, funky, rocky times,
They'll hide in sneak, or look, have a sneak peek,
Oh and Hazel Woody, little cutie, cuddly,
Eek be careful! Got little spikes!
Adventures go on and on like a happy song,
Fruit and vegetables, munch, crunch, munch bunch,
Fun paw prints, all the way,
Here, there and everywhere.

Lorraine

You're a bright star, fun, cool,
You're like a warm hug,
Almost like another mum to us all,
Though she baked cakes,
Christmas cake was her most famous one,
Loved music/movies, chirpy, dynamic personality.
She felt to me like an Agatha Christie creation of Miss Marple,
Her music was great taste,
Loved her whisky or brandy,
Oh dear me, not at the same time though.

Cats & Dogs

Meow, meow said the cat in the hat,
Meow, meow said the cat who hates hats,
But wears a cravat.
Woof, woof, said Mr Woolf of Derbyshire
Who wears a monocle and a large hat,
"I don't like cats" said Mr Woolf,
"Well i don't like dog's" says Simone,
Well jolly dolly the persian cat with
Alively sneer, purrfect glance said
"Can we get on and always try to get along?
Be wise and purrfect.
We are cats and dogs, help each other
Then chase each others tails, that'll be hell".

Valentines Day

Valentines day its here again,
Oh wow!
Be loved or in love,
Will you be their valentines heart?
Don't grow apart.
Chocolates, flowers, sweets,
Presents for loved ones, all the way.
There will be romances, proposals,
Happy and spontaneous in their way,
Plus hope to make their day.
But Mr St Valentine was a busy matchmaker,
A busy bumbling, fuzzy bee,
But card shops become the idols and ideas,
They're the romantic creatives.

Wonky Donkey

Wonky Donkey, feels like a funny word,
Crazy, dazey, hazey sound, but it's the meaning of it,
Feels when are good or about to fall down,
Becomes crazy, that's why it's a wonky donkey situation.
Sometimes things go right or wrong, poor donkey,
Hope he's not drunk and gone all wonky.

First Kiss

First kiss, eh kind of feel good,
Anxious, strange, thou is
Mesmorising, funny, hilarious
That sets your tummy in somersaults or knots
Or even nervy windy issues.
Thy first kiss is an extremely odd ball feeling,
It's a melancholic mellowy feeling
When you kiss for the very first time.
It's like loss of pain, body likes to chill,
Warm, chill and at ease or your body shuts down,
Gives you a deep breath, warm, fuzzy sensation, numb lips.
Alas, those unkissable lips that sink,
Your mind goes flop – flip flop,
Knotty, soothing reaction,
It's like a kind of magic trick that goes quick.

Jelly & Ice Cream

Jelly and ice cream is a magical supreme dream,
It's for clowns alike,
But for parties and birthdays
Or just after a grand sunday lunch, brunch.
Yum yummy.
That cold sensational feeling,
That heavenly whirl in a swirl,
Like an adventurous sundae of cream, fruit, nuts and chocolate.
Ice cream, sweet, yellowy, cool as ice,
Though nice with wibbly, wobbly, fruitful, wobbly jelly.

Jam & Toast

Jam and toast is always a grand host,
Fit for a King or Queen,
Princess, Prince or even Dukes or Countess.
Jam is sweet, lively,
Toast for a great host or mistress
Or hostess with the mostess
Crunch, munch.
The toaster like a funny motor,
It angles the bread to toast, turn in an old toaster,
Roasts it, gives it a brown, malty, crunchy munchie day!
Lovely with tea, delightful, magical,
Jam and toast, many versions,
Many variations of flavours.

Cadbury's Dairy Milk

Oh the texture on the mixture,
The heavenly sweet friend,
It's a milky chocolate treat.
It's a lively and lovely creamy feeling,
Like a river of chocolate and cocoa beans of a flowy time,
Shiny, happy chocolatey bars.
All kinds of different chocolates,
Flake, bars, milk tray, yum,
Fruit and nut, many more.
Super cool and delicious.

Hippos

Hippo's are extremely weird but funny animals.
They make the most strange noises,
Big teeth that crunches.
Love mud pits, stay and swim,
But do they smile?
Thats why they're called 'Hungry Hippos'.
They make noises filled of wet, swimming, laughing,
As cool as smelly wellies.
Bless. They're funny, smiley, hungry hippos.

The Undateables

The Undateables is a must see TV programme.
It's a thought provoking, very educational,
Kooky, eccentric, melancholic,
Tea for two or for three, cheery, bright, sometimes funny,
Delightfully dynamic.
It's creative with art, poetry, sports, daredevil extreme sports,
It's clever, the name, but it's not a nice thing or name,
Will it be the same?
It's B.A.F.T.A. nominated many times, it should win one day.
The episodes are cool, chillaxing, breezy,
Momentous and serenading.
Quotes, wit, wisdom cheering on are top notch notes,
Or a quick magical trick, quick don't blink,
It's a great show on Channel 4,
All I can say is funtastic!

Ode To First Dates

It's a great fun packed, enchanted,
Will they, won't they?
Seeing many couples come and go to the restaurant,
What a way to wine and dine,
Oh so great company, lively, lovely, they'll be fine.
Some work and some don't,
But least they have a chance again for a lucky second date.
They're kooky, eccentric, creative, quirky,
But it's always a waiting game, dating.
Humourous, spontaneous, quirky, magical
Sparkling show on Channel 4,
A must for romantics out there.
Love is an odd thing sometimes
Is love fair?
Though it's need it's joy
But it always comes and goes,
Hope this series stays on and on.

Autumn Leaves

Autumn leaves are floaty and fall as mist
Filled likes sunny tomorrow, smiles and treasures.
Oh the leaves of bittersweet green morphing into a spruce of
Natural redheaded colours of red, orange, yellow, limey fluorescent,
Oh leaves turn into copper, gold and russet,
Pure clocks of time, so everything's fine.
Leaves fall from the sky, acorns fly,
Pirouette below like a trembling tree, they glide,
The pitter patter of change,
Do leaves like change? NO! It's an outrage.
It's like a charismatic quench of nuttyness, squirrels, conquer their food
With it's fists, trying to get nuts as it's wary of food,
Or does it like cheese and onion crisps?
Because one stole my packet and ate them, blooming cheek!
So that's Autumn for now,
Hope it's cool, eccentric, creative flair, colours of radiant glow,
As Autumn's colours show.

An Ode to Bath

She is a song from the quaint years, the melodies, the lyrics.
The scenic views and forests, villages,
The journeys, like an amazing discovery of the past,
How times have passed, oh it's gone so fast.
The romans came and lived and conquered, hence the baths.
In Bath film and TV have been filmed here,
Oh cheery, bright and fair.
Bath is magnificent. It has memories like treasures,
Many splendid adventures.
Tea and cakes, oh yummy scrummy,
Delightful for your tummy.
Memories that take you back for more?
Bath is a rare and quirky quaint and bubbly of past times like the Georgian and Victorian era.
The town, the view, the routes to the countryside are always by heart,
That never want to grow apart.
The houses in a circle, like a 360 spin, like a whirlwind.
Oh they're magic, sweets, tea rooms galore,
The Jane Austin Museum, find pubs, clubs,
Restaurants are full, wine and dine.
Oh and a night out at an evening with Shaine and friends.
Bath is a friend you can depend,
It's sweet, sassy, cool and versatile.
Thank you Bath for having me!!

Isla Fisher

Wow, a divine, fab, quirky actress,
All the way from Summer Bay,
Home and Away,
But now a cool, funny lady of comedy, serious films.
Her film roles are a shopaholic, a magician, bachelorette,
Romantic comedies.
She likes everyones remedy.
A red head, aw so foxy, charismatic,
Creative aspect on presence on screen.
She's joyful, mesmerising quality, what's next for her?
Well known for films, she's kooky but really funny.
A wonderful captivating artist of film and TV.
Hope she works here in Britain for great films.
A smile, possibly working in theatre.
I wonder if she likes a decent cup of tea or coffee.

Oh Candy

Oh Candy it's sweet.
It's a must, oh it's a treat though,
They are delicious to eat,
Alas, it's a sugar rush.
The sweetness,
The texture,
The hollow feature.
Sweets come in all sorts of sizes, shapes, colours,
Pastilles, fruit juices are in. Yummy scrummy feeling.
Liquorice, Mints, Riccolas, Pear Drops,
Starburst, boiled sweets, is sure a hit,
Oh Candy, sweet n sugary.
Tastes cool (goodness or naughty),
Too much sweets, Oh eat me!!
Chocolates are delightful and beautiful like serenading a song.
Both sweets come together in all factories.
Mums, yay, or great rotisserie sweet off.
Treats and sweets from the past that take you back for more
Or take you back from your youthful days of sweet treats.
Memories of buying chocolates for your loved ones of
Milk Tray or Black Magic or even Dairy Box.

Aww what about Galaxy? Oh yum,
The Flake ads, Cadburys Flake girls - they rock.

Candy can be a girls name.
Sadly I don't know a Candy but I know a Julie,
But never mind.
The sweetest thing is honey and busy bees
To make all sweet things sticky and runny.

Clocks

Oh how time beats a second, oh damn it,
Blasted clock, it's stopped!
Bugger it, now feel like a twit.
As it's strange though as time, clock hands,
Oh let's synchronise our watches and start again,
Oh crumbs, it's like a murder mystery.
Fob watches, father time clocks, vintage wall clocks,
The sound of tick tock could be dangerous,
Hearing tick tock, oh the alarms!
But sometimes clocks go silent,
And days, weeks, years are going faster.
Have time.
But what if time just stopped a bit?
Then it becomes travelling in time,
Oh wowzers, that'd be cool supreme,
Won't time be calm.
Days of wonder feels an array of humour and strange life,
Time is so old,
Has it gone bold?
Time is a mature age and feeling,
But deja vu feelings like you're getting groundhog days,
Ahh, make your day un in all sorts of ways.

The Snowman That Likes To Ski

On a near planet called Christmas,
Where snow happens quite often, parties happen.
Chilly days, happy dances, memorable sways.
There on this white blanket of snowy planet
Is a snowman that likes to ski, who likes Brie,
He likes to go and ski down slopes.
Does he get a frost adrenaline rush,
That goes up to his white snowy cheeks?
Be careful, too much adrenaline could be the melt of him,
And sadly wouldn't be nice for him.
He wouldn't be so cheeky and bright.
So he decided to do work with ice cream,
That was mainly his to do with, or dream.

A Revolution

A revolution of things is written in the stars,
Election day is here to roam.
The thing is, is who to choose?
What will they say or do?
All want to fight for us all.
We don't want to be betrayed,
That wouldn't go right or nice for us all.
We want their words to stick right out and be counted
And say what there going to do,
Mean every word, otherwise there would be
Mass hysteria and bleak darkness,
That certainly wouldn't be timeless or exciting.
So, a revolution, put all things back to normal,
Hope the government listens what we do,
If they don't hypnotise them.
And that's just being silly that is.
But you never know.

Dreams Within A Dream

What if you awake from a nightmare or eerie dream,
Have you had any cheese the night before?
Are you running?
Are you dreaming?
Are you sinking?
Are you shouting?
Are you screaming?
Are you hiding thing's or someone,
Or terrors of the night?
What if you're dreaming when you're woken up
But still dreaming within a dream?
Oh that's eerie, weary, really daunting.
Haunting, is it a ghost, a host?
That's scary.
Is it an alien?
Is it possible?
Is it just fear, strange, fiery, place to dream?
Is there source or power?
Is it monsters or dream creatures drinking your knowledge and thirst
Like pockets of memory?
Eek, pretty eerie and scary.
Bleak, dark, dismal.
Do we get out of dreaming?

Do we stop it, chant it, surround it, destroy it, leave it?
Oh god no, be efficiently, terrifying, shocking.
Do we have to think to erase the vile, fearful dreams
Of wise enigmatic bright, happy dreams?
Like a cloud of beams, cheeky and bright.
Is it floating dreams in mid air?
That's lovely and fair, gentle and bright,
A lot of fun and care.

Love Thou Is Strange

Love is like a planet of fear,
We go for goals, come back for cheer.
Love thou is strange, love is like music serenading a note,
We come back for some air, go there to gasp for that curly, twirly feeling.
Love is bland, creative eccentric,
Love is grand, it's hollow like a melancholic bundle of joy.
But when you lose love, loss it's an odd,
Sad feeling that makes you down,
Never frown, you're like you're falling down
A hole or a well or surroundings.
That isn't nice, it's black, bleak darkness eats away,
Like it's going for a play in every way,
But you get over it, sometimes not, but try before you buy.
Go, I believe in you. Ladies and girls, find love,
Don't be lost in love,
Have spirit, be brave, carry on.
But truth is, love is a planet of fear,
We go for gold and goals, though we come back for more and cheer.
Be bright as a star,
Give love a sign and a well mellow jeer,
Be cool, be yourself, bright, no tears, no fears.

What If

What if you knew you met that one, you laugh, you joked,
Chemistry setting in, but get on so well,
But a mind blowing sensation becomes a flow, but saw humour, laughter,
Oh, that blossoms into a blow.
Oh no, not ye thine bumble of bother.
She says she's with someone, oh no, pooh sticks,
Heart goes bang, fears drift in like lost soul,
Have you all ever been in a situation like that?
Bit of a pooh sticks situation. What do you do?
Best to leave and go, not ruin it.
It's sometimes like and echo from the past,
But are the ones there in a relationship happy?
Do they treat their partners, girlfriends well?
Then isn't it blooming great and swell.
But the real man thing to do is to walk away and say goodbye,
Say farewell.
Funny about what if's, there's always that saying,
Well, what if? What if?
Or possibly the changes and choices are of what if,
The time is to walk away,
Say hello, and she says goodbye,
Goodbye. Bye.
Never mind, though that's hard to walk away,
I wasn't chicken or crazy, or didn't want to play away,
Don't believe in cheating, it rocks it badly.

Natalie Wood

A dark haired beauty, iconic actress of wisdom was she,
A mysterious screen icon, was as Maria in West Side Story.
Pretty eyes, oh heavenly, magical, stunning, fair, maiden, air,
Like a fresh lady of bliss, red kissable lips,
Soul, soothing, anticipating.
A temptress by night or like a Lady Godiva by dusk,
Sweet american rosebud, she's a kindred spirit full of praise,
Oh she's ace.
An actress by trade, mission, maybe a magical star,
So bright, dynamic, stunner, that would have gone on so far.
But tragedy struck and she was killed in an accident at sea in 1983,
The world was shell shocked,
Devastated as a nation, for in a life's desert rose of beauty creation.
Her looks and wisdom did show,
Would make men go weak under the knees,
Wonder if the lady of films was a precious soul,
So refreshing and revitalising to see.

Ava Gardner - A Truly Timeless Screen Goddess

Ava, a bright star, so pretty in mystery, suspense or thriller,
A siren that looks like charismatic dream,
Lovely as bright as I'd ever seen.
Brilliant, heavenly actress, top of the game, pretty eyes,
So powerful like a code of eternity or let something
Flair out of destiny written in the stars.
Was she of Princess or enigma, scent of autumn or summer breeze?
Though beauty did she, thou is true of the heart,
Many films she did do, and some did part,
Some might have been in horse and cart,
Historical or cowboy westerns or involved in relationships
That went or crumbled or drifted,
A time that wanted maybe to forget.
Her film roles were gracious like sugar and wine one seductress,
Essence of melancholy, or surreal, like it's a dream,
Ava foretells the wind, the seasons flow.
Actress,
Clever temptress,
Like a princess of an arabian adventure, banging chic,
And passion for fashion.

She may have been a diva or a lovely funtastic empress of the film world,
Priceless in all our thoughts.
You're a goddess of many talented films that stand the test of time,
In all times and curvacious signs, an american beauty,
Wise, cracking, so charm, cool, a shimmer collection.
Movie memorabilia, is the gift of love.

The Penny Farthing Bicycle

Take a trip down memory lane,
Through a trip in the past,
This is a funny looking bicycle, it is known as a Penny Farthing.
It's Victorian, the front wheel is huge,
It is high above the ground,
This bicycle was truly hard to ride,
It's different and unique from a bygone era,
The small wheel is right at the back,
It's got a funny shaped seat,
Have you ever ridden one?
Back then other people laughed at them,
Because as it was huge to ride,
A lot of Victorians & Edwardians fell over or off it,
Some couldn't just get on with it or on top of it as the wheel was so high.
The smaller other wheel was tiny and little.
But alas a bygone era, it was a mode of transport
To get by 'to and fro'.
Back then I think now, it can be tricky or easy
Depending on your balance and stamina,
But oh for adventure they look like antique types now.
But still test the time now as they need a comeback.
I'd like to be on one of them to ride up and down,
But only if I was great at riding a bike still.

Things That Go Bump In The Night - Are They Alive?

You know when you watch a classic horror film
American horror or English Hammer,
And watch a timeless monster feature, creature,
Dracula and Frankenstein,
Do they survive, multiply or morph? What's their air, their supply?
Their fun or frustration?
Are they alive?
But why or what, they're walking like the dead, their hideout or lair.
When a soothsayer, villager or know it all says
"Don't go into the woods or castles that are cursed with fear",
Unknown fear to the unquiet dead,
Is it the castles that look beautiful but one, gothic like eerie places,
But you listen to the villager but then you say
"Don't talk nonsense" or "Don't be a fool",
Then the mystery deepens and horror, fear and mayhem begins.
So darkness left no power,
There creatures and monsters desire of their party guests.
Do they survive or be revived as then?
But when thing's aint there before,
Noises or unknown faces or deadlier sounds,
Do they have time to be kept alive, not so magical,

But grim and darkness for Count Dracula, fang's, wit and sheer delight,
Be careful of love bites,
Frankenstein just want's a friend or mate or even a date,
But there looks abound, are sure to be a fright, fierce,
Be daunting pre image of loss, sadness, one looks,
Werewolves howling through the strange moonlit night.
Be careful of fangs from a woman's bite, sharp teeth,
As blood curdling dreams,
Mostly Dracula's reign is his beef,
Though be careful of thy eyes following you or looking at you or your every move through a painting,
Be careful in the mist and darkness and despair,
Be very careful out there, be sure, be alert,
But do survive, be alive,
Don't get revived.

The Sky At Night

Oh twas the sky at night,
Such a delight
From the very beginning in '57,
A mesmerising feel of eccentric sounds of the universe,
It meets a whirlwind discovery of science fiction.
Twas the sky at night,
Wonderful sight,
Seeing a cascade of surreal colours,
Urban red, yellow, orange.
Scientists and fans of star gazing having fun,
Drinking tea from flasks with their companion.

Time

Time is portal pockets of discovery, it's rare, so precious, spontaneous,
It's strange, it's an outrage.
Why doesn't time stop to think and stand still?
Let it freeze, just chill.
Oh it goes when you're having alot of fun, but when you're doing nothing it slows down.
It's got it's perks and quirks, magic moments,
Sometimes the feeling of time is a weird n weary meltdown.
It makes days frown, let comedy be the clown,
Let it be time, be crowned.
Just imagine if time could just stop, think, cease time itself,
But time is a tricky device, a strange thing,
Whoever thought of time, very creative.
Hope there be time travel one day, hmm I wonder,
Across the moon and stars and below.
Come on time, it's time!
Be friendly not an evil curse or strange rhyme or a fast flow of timeline.
Time can it be rewritten? Strange as it seems, sand beams,
It's a funny, odd feeling,
Time is unique, skillful, beautiful,
Maybe time is a woman.
I think so, possibly, that'd be cool. The best thing that time can be.

The TARDIS

The TARDIS, an awesome craft of technology crafted by the Doctor,
Who stole a type 40 police box from Gallifrey
And landed in 76 Totters Lane in London, a junkyard.
The Doctor No.1 met Ian and Barbara for a reason
About his granddaughters behaviour at Coal Hills school.
The Doctor thought Ian and Barbara were spying on them.
And then they were whisked off to another time and world.
Adventures were born.
The TARDIS is a mysterious magical blue box.
It stands for Time And Relative Dimensions In Space.
Also it matches it's surroundings has a particular worry on the Doctor,
The chameleon circuit blends in.
Whenever danger strikes or erupts,
Its cloister bell, hums, bums and drums it's soul.
Or if it's been knocked out or gassed or shot at,
It has got a button to tell it to materialise some place else,
Near or far.

If I Were A Timelord

If I were a timelord,
I'd take you on adventures through time and space,
See the world in a different light,
Thwart monsters, aliens that want to threaten
Or rule the world or destroy it.
NOOO, Don't do that, let's talk, a way to ease and reassure the villains.
Oh, if I were a timelord,
I'd take you on adventures if you were bored.
Maybe on Earth, modern day or before, or way, way, way back.
As really me, the doctor, was bored and stole a TARDIS on Gallifrey
Before landing in 1963.
Be aware as most enemies or timelords are good or bad or on the run.
Well we can have excitement and fun.
Defeat Daleks, oh yes! Cybermen, Zygons, Sea Devils, Silurians
Sil, the delightful Mechanoids & the sweet but deadly Kandyman.
Many more sinister pacts of the Meddling Monk, or even the
Celestial Toymaker, plus the many faces of the Master and now Missy.
So step aboard my companion/or companions, welcome aboard.
You'll have a wicked sense of fun and adventure,
And a great wardrobe of clothes, there we go!!! Great times.
Im the Doctor! And we'll thwart baddies, monsters,
Treasures,
See the stars,
Drink tea,
But be warned I may regenerate,
But don't worry it's still me!

The Fisher King

The Fisher King is an awesome piece of monster, a villainous idea.
Wow, a creative, busy, cool and calm idea.
Oh the fear,
The roaring jeers.
The Fisher King is a thought provoking enemy
In the doctors time stream.
Oh my word it's a tall kind of species character.
Seven feet tall, awesome villainous creature on screen.
Though sadly it didn't have much screen time,
But oh my word the roar, the scream,
The edginess of the shore sea creature.
The Fisher King is also like wild, strange creatures.
Were they like sea devils or related?
Or were they relations I wonder?
As the flood happened the Fisher King was swept and flushed away.
Do you think he escaped
To defeat the Doctor once more for revenge again?
Maybe, who knows!
Will have to see, umm won't we!

The Weeping Angels

Statues of death.
Never look back or blink,
Your heart might sink,
You'd be zapped or transported back in time 'til you die.
Strange, made by stone. Such a classy, top notch fright fest of golden treasured memories of the 10th, 11th doctors to defeat,
Wow an inventive, gutsy,
Wibbly, wobbly,
Timey, wimey
Creatures of stone.
Flesh and fear.
For goodness sake don't blink,
You may be gone and your heart might sink,
Zapped out of the unknown into different time periods.
They're not easy to defeat.
Our friend Sally Sparrow first encountered these gargoyle statues of death and forces of evil.
They look frightening but also beautiful in one way.
They took away the doctors friends,
Amy and Rory Pond into 1930's Manhattan,
And took them again as they blinked and didn't bat an eyelid.
NOOOOOOOOOO!
Gone but not forgotten.

Amy did say goodbye raggedy man, goodnight.
Will these devil incarnate monsters of magical creature
Come back for more?
They'd sure enjoy it all and take someone else.
It'll be their ball.

Dementia & Alzheimers

Dementia. What is it? What, why?
Is it a ghost from someones past acting as their host?
It's like a shadow of here, there or lost in limbo between the past.
Black and white era.
Mainly it's memory loss, or pain of knowing who you are,
What you do anymore.
So elegantly strained, sad though, need help, hope,
Dementia care and friendly people that has time to help.
But not stare, just care.
Though, alas music and drama, combination of therapy
Help the mind at calm and ease.
Makes them proud and pleased to remember who they are in life,
They remember or did in a life so far.
So what's the difference between Alzheimers and Dementia?
What causes the memory to go? What, when, why?
I Shaine Singer the poet, writer and actor will find out why.
Before a sigh or even say, I will help find out if there is a case study.
Make it calm and go steady, not rock bottom.
Stamp out dementia or even Alzheimers.
Understand it, come on now, let's make a band, that'll be sound.
I will show you the ropes and see what care is there.
They don't want to go without, it's like going to memory lane

Where memories never fade.

But when this friction of sorrow or illness, it's a horrible mess.

Can it be fiction one day instead of a fact?

So let music, old films, soundtracks,

Classical music take your memory, just go with the flow.

Way, way back to fond memories in your memories.

Take a box of delights, so bright, of a happy glowy smile, essence.

A radiant glimmer of HOPE

With something to help and cope.

Raise money for charities to help proceeds.

I think there's a cure and HOPE.

Educate.

Kate Beckinsale

My word, she is devine, heavenly goddess.
Like wow, amazing.
Thy screen siren from the past, beautiful but looks radiant,
Lively with a happy filmic smile.
She is elegant like an english rose, that may like a pose.
She played another siren of the big screen, Ava Gardner in the film of
Leonardo DiCaprio. Of Howard Marks, 'The Aviator'.
She was cute, sweet, ravashing, with sharp, delicate, angel,
Like a belle of the ball.
In the film she looked very much like Ava,
Stunning, like seeing double. But what an actress, so lovely.
In all genres Kate is a wonderful sweet name.
Her eyes are a sight to soothe in a light.
She's a professional, funtastic, essential, actress
Learns her roles in all kinds of acting.
Awesome and as fresh as a daisy, like a girl with a flower in her hair.
So rare in beauty. She takes a breath away like raindrops
Come clashing down, every cloud.
Smart as a cookie, but definitely a cutie.
Everytime you see her in the movies they're exciting, thrilling,
Racey or sets your heartbeats in a pace.
If I had a chance i'd love to work with her or meet her, oh yes please.
I'd be at mellow and at ease.

She was great, anticipating goddess in the Underworld films
As a vampire slayer, werewolf slayer, aww lovely in rubber.
Crikey, it would make your heartbeat pace and dance
Like you're doing a routine of Samba.
Has an everlasting effect in film makers psyche.
With class, poise, elegance and grace as a fair lady,
Whatever films she will do or has done,
Getting all sorts of parts.
Film is an art.
She is funky, beauty from the north,
She is groovy in the heart.

Zygons

A sharp monster, a race of dominated species.
So bloodthirsty and razor tooth, enigmatic design.
The Zygons first created by Robert Banks Stewart back in the 1970's,
They were thrilling and dangerous.
Bodysnatchers that morph into somebody else and steal another body.
Wuite a fascinating race of darkness.
Shape shifters they have a piercing scream whilst they're on screen.
Their roar is unique.
They're a strange invention of creature.
They're like shaped monsters with tentacles on a hook, or suckers.
They make squealy screechy screams,
They love to hide away in cellars, underwater bases.
They're scary looking monsters.
Are out for revenge again, an invasion,
Plus a Zygon Inversion to populate the world.
Oh my Doctor, be careful on this, be very wise and try and solve an idea.
What an enemy. An evil like species. Another threat.
Has the doctor got a chance to thwart their plans I wonder?
Yes of course!
Will they show help or remorse?
Find out whether the invasion of Zygons can be indeed put a stop to it.
Their voices are quite enticing, creepy.
Dangerous creatures,
Awesome features.

The Avengers

A cult psychedelic T.V classic series of spies,
Britishness, eerie sci-fi or spy-fi.
Fantastic series, memorable guest casts.
John Steed, another character as well back in 1961,
When it all began but the actor was Ian Hendry.
Then came Cathy Gale, Emma Peel, Tara King.
After that in mid late 1970's Purdey and Gambit, also with John Steed.
All played wonderfully well by Patrick MacNee, Ian Hendry,
Honor Blackman, Dame Diana Rigg, Linda Thorson,
Joanna Lumley, Gareth Hunt.
Then film version with Ralph Fiennes it tried before it buyed.
Aw the costumes, like out of a dream, something of the unknown.
Leather catsuits of Cathy Gale and Emma Peel,
Kind of a fantasy then, still is to this day.
Whats your thought's on the series?
The fights, wit, humour, villains,
Calm, cool, collected, english gentlemen
With a very hard steel bowler hat.
Robotic forms, robots arms that swing and knock you out
Flying or all things in sight.
Something of an imagination or clones,
Mystery of all things scientist and science.
Was it fantasy or reality?

Somethings are now science fact,

Was it a quality perfect show, created by Brian Clemens?

Was it a pact though, it's a spy-fi with a difference,

Drama, cool, quirky, vibrant show, it was a lot sometimes, quite violent.

Fantastic series, always thought of a cult TV classic exquisite.

The theme tune is mesmerising, and in awe.

Sunday Roasts

Ahh Sunday roasts.
The smells and scents of the kitchen,
Of all mums and dads
Preparing the food that's so glorious
Mouthwatering too.

Catch ups sat at the dinner tables
Dinner's, roasts for your hosts.
Chicken, pork, beef, lamb, turkey,
Or dinner for one, or team up finds
Family at a country pub, or your local.

Sunday roasts are cool, quirky, timeless traditions.
Here's to a wonderful Sunday roast.

Shrove Tuesday

Shrove Tuesday, yeah, pancake day.
Wow, what fun, pitter patter pancake.
You can have sweet and savoury
Gorgeous in every other way.
All things nice.
You can use it as a side dish or a big meal
Or even as a just a meal.
Only problem is pancakes on the ceiling
Or even on the floor.
Plus it can be a messy, fabulous time
With the batter mix, it's kinda bliss.

If I Were King for a Day

If I were king for a day
I'd give the nation some hospitality.
Help third world countries get their lives back on track.
Make people smile and laugh
Make a National Laughter day, in every other way.
I'll stand out and stamp out war!!
As it's blumin' not good for no flaming cause.
Haven't they learned their lessons?
War is no fun. It's deadly.
Makes it for deadlier, power mad conspirators.
Help work with the government.
Repair all things.
Stop things from going wrong.
That's why I'd be king for a day.
Make a speech and have my say.

Fun at the Fair

Oh the fun of the fair.
Roll up, roll up, welcome to the fun fair.
Where fun flows everywhere.
Ode to the fun fair
Where rides glide fast 'n' slow
Or pirhouette or go upside down or inside out.
Where the Hall of Mirrors shroud in mystery.
Alas, the ghost train, be prepared to be spooked
With the hairs of the chest, oh er!
The food of ones delight
Burgers, hot dogs, sweet treats,
Toffee apples, popcorn or chocolate.
So welcome, oh and have fun at the fair.
Meet and greet with friends or loved ones,
Or a date or a night at the fair.

Four Leaf Clover

Four leaf clover is like the span and life of the party of Ireland
All the treasures of scenic views and hill sides, places, are a must.
A four leaf clover is a map of all things green, mellowy yellowy feel.
Does a clover have a taste or a scent as maybe like a herb?
Oh ye wonderful sweet natured green friend.
You little fluourescent green span of something
A marvel gem of emerald green,
Beautiful picturesque views I've ever seen.
I'll always think of Ireland.

Hallowe'en

Welcome to Hallowe'en, where spooks, ghosts, ghouls,
Goblins, wizards and witches come to play.
Things that go bump and pfft in the night.
Fears of eerie music and monsters.
Hail the night, ohh, ahh
What a sight before spooky, kooky Hallowes Eve.

The costumes look surreal and almost like real,
Where it's a whirlwind dream
Blood red ink or paint or someone elses.
Where events and parties gather all round and together.

Welcome to Hallowe'en
It'll be a scream of bloodthirsty delights.
Remember it's only jolly good scenes.
But hope there's no screen queens
Enjoy the night if you don't like Hallowe'en.
Be safe and sound.
Take care.
Enjoy yourselves
And get home safe.

Love Bugs

Love bugs are a fuzzy soothing sensation
That is almost like a chemical feeling.
Pure conversation.
Do you get them when you fall for someone?
They're a bit like heart shaped gems
Or funny twist and turn inside out,
Like a butterfly, gliding, flowing,
Higher and higher.

But sometimes we learn from this
Not to rush in,
Them stomach or heart sings
Or feels something different.
It's like sweet things that sparkle throughout.

Sometimes love bugs make you feel lost,
Or can't eat or sleep, can't think straight.
Oh you devilishly love bugs.

Laughter

Laughter is a strange thing
Funny chemicals, it's a childhood thing
See what makes the nation laugh.
I think humour needs to be on the NHS.
Sometimes we only see comedy laughter
When we watch it on TV or see it live.
In music hall times like The Good Old Days
Even mostly new is theatre, sitcoms.
Canned laughter is when shows are on
Underneath is the laughter for the jokes.
Slapstick is my thing.
What's yours?

The Big Yellow Duck

Quack, quack, quack says the big yellow duck.
The big yellow duck is a cool dude.
Bright, smiley, cheerful as the yellowy sun
Who likes to have a lot of fun.

He's calm and sophisticated when he has eggs on toast.
He could be a brilliant host.
You could have toast
With the host.

The big yellow duck,
Crackers, eccentric, creative,
Likes a splish splash
In the bath.

Likes television afterwards
With a big cup of tea
And some bird seed
Covered in chocolate.

The Man on the Moon

"Houston", do we have a problem?
People in space.
Space men or women,
It's called the space race.

One giant leap for mankind
All the history of space
Sets our hearts at a pace.
Now we've had a hero
Who has been in space.

I've always dreamt when I was little,
What we did at weekends when back to school,
I would write that I've been on the moon.
To find some cheese.

See what's on Mars
But one thing
These people are stars.
Great starmen and starwomen.

The Naughty Christmas Elf

Twas one night before Christmas
There in Elfland lived Eric the Elf,
Who liked to misbehave.

He liked Christmas a lot
But whilst making toys
He'd mess them up.
Tweak them, change them,
Unwrap presents, naughty Eric.
What a naughty Elf he is.

Until one day on Christmas Day morning
He was told to stop messing around,
Behave and put things right,
So he ended up going into stand up comedy
In the new year.
Or try prank comedy
To find a better remedy.

The Pig in the Wig

The pig in the wig
Liked to dress well
Like a Hollywood starlet
In a blonde wig.
The pig in the wig
A razzle dazzle
Likes to party and to boogie
Loves a bit of champagne
She's not Miss Piggy
But friends with.
Her name is Cherie P
Loves to dance, hence to trance
But friendly in her pig sty
But her family don't always praise her
But they hope she'll do well.
As she dreams to make it big.
So she wants to be remembered as
The pig in the wig.
Be remembered as Cherie P.

Other Titles by Shaine Singer

The Book of Shaine

A Cup of Verbal Tea

Made in the USA
Coppell, TX
21 June 2021

57830089R10039